Loving Together

Sexual Enrichment Program

by
Lonnie Barbach, Ph.D.

ERECTION CONTROL WORKBOOK

ISBN: 87630-856-6 Erection Control Workbook

ISBN: 87630-854-X Sexual Desire Workbook
ISBN: 87630-855-8 Ejaculation Control Workbook
ISBN: 87630-857-4 Discovering Orgasm Workbook
ISBN: 87630-853-1 Therapist's Manual

Published by
BRUNNER/MAZEL, INC.
A member of the Taylor & Francis Group
47 Runway Road, Suite G
Levittown, PA 19057-4700

Manufactured in the United States of America

10 9 8 7 6 5 4 3 2

TABLE OF CONTENTS

iv

INTRODUCTION

Every man occasionally has difficulty obtaining or maintaining an erection. Problems with getting or maintaining erections are very common and have many different causes.

For some men, erection difficulties are the result of a physiological problem—where constriction of the blood supply prevents sufficient blood from entering the penis to create an erection. Sometimes the veins do not shut off completely and, much like a balloon with a slow leak, the penis does not remain rigid. It is also unreasonable for a man in his fifties and beyond to expect his penis to function exactly as it did when he was in his early twenties, or to assume he will automatically have an erection when he is tired, just doesn't feel aroused, or when he is angry with his partner. His penis may be saying "no" when he is unable to.

The Loving Together: Erection Control Program consists of 12 weeks of exercises that will teach you in a step-by-step fashion to better attain and maintain your erections as well as enabling you to have enjoyable and satisfying sex even on those occasions when you do not have an erection.

Some of the necessary skills will be taught first through masturbation. Afterward, partner exercises are outlined so that you can transfer the skills you have learned to lovemaking with your mate.

Since no sexual difficulty can be considered in a vacuum, exercises have been included each week to enhance the level of communication and the positive feeling toward your partner. While these form the foundation for intimacy outside the bedroom, they affect sexual satisfaction as well. There are also exercises that deal with increasing your awareness of pleasure in general—something that, given our Puritan culture, many of us are not very skilled at. Finally, there are pencil and paper activities designed to enable you to think about your sexuality and to assess some of your unique needs which can then be communicated to your partner.

For the best results, you will need to devote approximately three to four 20- to 30-minute blocks of time each week in order to complete the homework. While the program ideally fits into a three-month period, some couples or individuals who are too busy to complete the necessary assignments each week, will require extra time. It is important that you follow the exercises in order and complete each one successfully before going on to the next set of assignments, even if it means taking a couple of extra weeks to finish the program.

Spending significantly less than the three or four exercise sessions per week may not enable you to generate sufficient momentum to complete the program successfully. Positive experiences are built on positive experiences, but even unsuccessful attempts at the homework assignments offer important lessons in terms of what does not work and the way in which you may need to fashion your sexual relationship differently.

If there is anything I have learned from 23 years of doing sex therapy and marital counseling, it is that there is no one right way to have a successful intimate and sexual relationship. Each couple must devise the kind of lovemaking patterns that are the most satisfying for them. The fundamental purpose of following the exercises in this program is to enable you to do precisely that.

For more in-depth explanations and more complete coverage of the material, please read *The New Male Sexuality* by Bernie Zilbergeld, Ph.D. Dr. Zilbergeld's book also contains helpful hints for overcoming a variety of the common difficulties you may run into while attempting the exercises. A number of exercises in this program have been adapted from his work.

Sex is fun. Have a good time with the process. If an exercise doesn't work for you, change it so that it meets your needs more precisely. Again I urge you not to skip any of the exercises. They have all been included for a reason. Each one adds a bit to the totality of new learning that will enable you to have a fully satisfying sexual relationship.

WEEK 1

JOURNAL EXERCISE

Keep a journal over the next week in order to record your observations in the following three areas that tend to affect sexual satisfaction:
Feelings about yourself
Feelings about your partner
The explicit sexual contact that takes place

Feelings about yourself
How did you feel about yourself today?
Did you feel attractive or a bit homely?
Were you happy, sad, or angry about something?
Were you tired and under stress? Were you full of energy?
Did you handle some situation particularly well or did some interaction still bother you?

Rate from 1 to 10 (from terrible to great)

Feelings about your partner
Did you feel close to your partner?
Did you feel withdrawn and distant?
Did you feel criticized by your partner?
Did you think of your partner today in a loving way?
Did you have a fight? Did you make up?
Did you have any sexual thoughts regarding your partner?

Rate from 1 to 10 (from distant to close)

Explicit Sexual Contact
Interest and initiation
What led up to sex? How did you feel about that? Who initiated sex? Did that please you? Were you feeling close and affectionate? Or were you preoccupied with other things? Did you feel sexual or would you rather have said no?

Time and place

What time of day did you have sex? If at night, were you tired? If in the morning were you rushed? Were you afraid of disturbing others or of being interrupted? Where did you have sex? Were there any special preparations?

Sexual activities

Which sexual activities aroused you? Which did not? Was there enough kissing, touching, foreplay? Did you have oral sex? What intercourse position(s) did you use?

Thoughts and fantasies

Did your thoughts or feelings get in the way? Were you worried about your partner's pleasure? Were you concerned about being a good lover? Were you concerned about ejaculating too rapidly? Were you preoccupied or angry? Did you incorporate any sexual fantasies into lovemaking?

Arousal and satisfaction

Rate both your sexual arousal level and overall satisfaction with each lovemaking session. **Use a scale from 0–10. On the arousal scale: 0 = no arousal, 10 = high arousal. On the satisfaction scale: 0 = high dissatisfaction, 5 = neutral, 10 = high satisfaction.** Notice any patterns?

Keep the journal at your bedside and record your feelings at the end of each day or just after you wake up. Don't wait more than 24 hours to record your feelings; your memory can play tricks on you.

Avoid value judgements. Be careful not to label any behaviors, feelings, or attitudes as good or bad. Just try to note your observations.

SAMPLE JOURNAL ENTRIES

DIARY

DATE: *Tuesday, 1/5*

SELF: *Rated - 10. Felt great - got a raise today!*

PARTNER: *Rated - 9. Jeanne was very happy for me.*

SEXUAL CONTACT:

Time and place: *In bed around 11:30 pm. We spent about 1 hour together. I wasn't satisfied.*

Interest and initiation: *I initiated sex and felt very interested.*

Sexual activities: *I enjoyed having oral sex but felt anxious as I started to enter her. Missionary position was used.*

Thoughts and fantasies: *Sex on the beach in Hawaii! But when I lost my erection I felt sad and hopeless.*

Overall arousal = *5*   Overall satisfaction = *2*

DIARY

DATE: *Wednesday, 1/6*

SELF: *Rated - 7. Generally felt good.*

PARTNER: *Rated - 7. Normal day.*

SEXUAL CONTACT:

Time and place: *None*

Interest and initiation: _____

Sexual activities: _____

Thoughts and fantasies: _____

Overall arousal =   Overall satisfaction =

DIARY

DATE: _Thursday, 1/7_

SELF: _Rated .5. Felt kind of ho-hum. Nothing really going on._

PARTNER: _Rated .3. Annoyed. Barbara was late for dinner._

SEXUAL CONTACT:

Time and place: _In bed, late, around 1am. I was exhausted._

Interest and initiation: _Not interested — she initiated._

Sexual activities: _Not much foreplay. Didn't get an erection._

Thoughts and fantasies: _None. Wanted to sleep._

Overall arousal = _0_   Overall satisfaction = _0_

YOUR JOURNAL ENTRIES

DIARY

DATE: _____

SELF: _____

PARTNER: _____

SEXUAL CONTACT:

Time and place: _____

Interest and initiation: _____

Sexual activities: _____

Thoughts and fantasies: _____

Overall arousal = ____   Overall satisfaction = ____

Day 1

DIARY

DATE: _____

SELF: _____

PARTNER: _____

SEXUAL CONTACT:
   Time and place: _____

_____

   Interest and initiation: _____

_____

   Sexual activities: _____

_____

   Thoughts and fantasies: _____

_____

Overall arousal =   Overall satisfaction =

Day 2

DIARY

DATE: _____

SELF: _____

PARTNER: _____

SEXUAL CONTACT:
   Time and place: _____

_____

   Interest and initiation: _____

_____

   Sexual activities: _____

_____

   Thoughts and fantasies: _____

_____

Overall arousal =   Overall satisfaction =

Day 3

DIARY

DATE: _____

SELF: _____

PARTNER: _____

SEXUAL CONTACT:
  Time and place: _____
  _____

  Interest and initiation: _____
  _____
  _____

  Sexual activities: _____
  _____
  _____

  Thoughts and fantasies: _____
  _____

Overall arousal = _____   Overall satisfaction = _____

Day 4

DIARY

DATE: _____

SELF: _____

PARTNER: _____

SEXUAL CONTACT:
  Time and place: _____
  _____

  Interest and initiation: _____
  _____
  _____

  Sexual activities: _____
  _____
  _____

  Thoughts and fantasies: _____
  _____

Overall arousal = _____   Overall satisfaction = _____

Day 5

DIARY

DATE: _____

SELF: _____

PARTNER: _____

SEXUAL CONTACT:
  Time and place: _____

_____

  Interest and initiation: _____

_____

_____

  Sexual activities: _____

_____

_____

  Thoughts and fantasies: _____

_____

Overall arousal =   Overall satisfaction =

Day 6

DIARY

DATE: _____

SELF: _____

PARTNER: _____

SEXUAL CONTACT:
  Time and place: _____

_____

  Interest and initiation: _____

_____

_____

  Sexual activities: _____

_____

_____

  Thoughts and fantasies: _____

_____

Overall arousal =   Overall satisfaction =

Day 7

PLEASURE LIST

Most of us do our work very well—but we've forgotten how to have fun!

Make a list of simple activities that give you pleasure—like this:

1. Watching a favorite TV show

2. Buying flowers

3. Window shopping

4. Taking a long walk

5. Playing a game of tennis

6. Taking time to read the paper

7. Taking a leisurely bath

8. Eating chocolate chip cookies

List at least 10 items—the more, the better!

After you have made your list, carry out a few of the items on it every day for a week! Yes! Every day!

This may seem like an easy exercise but it can be surprisingly difficult for many people.

PLEASURE LIST

1. _____
2. _____
3. _____
4. _____
5. _____
6. _____
7. _____
8. _____
9. _____
10. _____

Day 1 _____ _____

_____

Day 2 _____ _____

_____

Day 3 _____ _____

_____

Day 4 _____ _____

_____

Day 5 _____ _____

_____

Day 6 _____ _____

_____

Day 7 _____ _____

_____

KEGEL EXERCISES FOR MEN

These exercises were developed by Dr. Arnold Kegel and can help to strengthen the pelvic muscles around the penis. They also increase blood flow to the penis which can be important since blood flowing into the penis causes the erection. Regularly practicing the Kegel exercises may help with erection problems and can result in stronger sensations experienced in the penis. Some men find that practicing the Kegel exercises lead to stronger and more pleasurable orgasms as well.

First determine exactly which muscles are the ones you need to work with. The way to do this is by stopping and starting the flow of urine the next time you are in the bathroom. The muscles you squeeze to do this are the muscles you will be exercising.

Squeeze/Release

Start by squeezing and releasing these muscles 5 times, twice a day. Increase by 5 contractions each day until you have worked up to 70 contractions a day (35 during each session).

Squeeze/Hold/Release

As you squeeze the muscles hold for a count of 3 and then release. Once again, begin with 10 contractions a day (5 during each session) and work up to 70 contractions a day (35 during each session).

For fun, and a bit more of a challenge, drape a washcloth over your erect penis and then do the Kegel exercises.

For best results, continue to do the Kegel exercises for the rest of your life.

KEEP A RECORD OF YOUR PROGRESS WITH THE
KEGEL EXERCISES

		Squeeze/Release *Number of Contractions*	**Squeeze/Hold/Release** *Number of Contractions*
Day 1	1st session	_____	_____
Date_____	2nd session	_____	_____
Day 2	1st session	_____	_____
Date_____	2nd session	_____	_____
Day 3	1st session	_____	_____
Date_____	2nd session	_____	_____
Day 4	1st session	_____	_____
Date_____	2nd session	_____	_____
Day 5	1st session	_____	_____
Date_____	2nd session	_____	_____
Day 6	1st session	_____	_____
Date_____	2nd session	_____	_____
Day 7	1st session	_____	_____
Date_____	2nd session	_____	_____
Day 8	1st session	_____	_____
Date_____	2nd session	_____	_____

APPRECIATIONS EXERCISE

For one week, take time every day to think of three things that you appreciated about your partner that day. Make sure to tell her or him before the end of the day!

SAMPLE
Jan 6   You made love even though you were tired.
           You went to the bank for me.
           You called just to say "hi".

Day 1 _____ _____
_____
_____

Day 2 _____ _____
_____
_____

Day 3 _____ _____
_____
_____

Day 4 _____ _____
_____
_____

Day 5 _____ _____
_____
_____

Day 6 _____ _____
_____
_____

Day 7 _____ _____
_____
_____

WEEK 2

SEXUAL SCRIPTING EXERCISE

As we grow up, many of us receive a sexual "script" from our parents and others that strongly influences our attitudes toward sexuality. Now might be the time to change the script to accommodate your present life and suit the grown man or woman you've become. For example, sometimes little girls are taught that sex is bad or little boys are told that masturbation is shameful. These feelings can linger on into adulthood and affect your sex life in negative ways. Take some time to think about your parents' attitudes toward sex, what they told you, and how you felt during these discussions, or how you felt about the lack of them. Try also to think about conversations you have had with friends, or what you have been taught by your religious upbringing.

Note which attitudes you consider positive and want to keep in your script. And note those attitudes that are negative and that you might want to change or drop from your script. Remember, you can direct your own life now!

My Personal History

Positive Attitudes:

_____
_____
_____
_____
_____
_____

Negative Attitudes:

_____
_____
_____
_____
_____
_____

CARING DAYS

Make a list of at least 10 things that your partner does, or could do for you that make you feel cared for—then add to the list each day. These should be small things like calling from work, kissing you good-bye, planning a night on the town, complimenting you on how you look. All the items on the list should be positive—what you would like your partner to start to do or continue to do, *not* what you want your partner to stop doing.

Caring Days List

1. _____
2. _____
3. _____
4. _____
5. _____
6. _____
7. _____
8. _____
9. _____
10. _____
11. _____
12. _____
13. _____
14. _____
15. _____
16. _____
17. _____
18. _____

Share your Caring Lists with each other and then post them on the refrigerator door or bathroom mirror as gentle reminders. **Carry out three of the items on your partner's list every day.**

What did you do today to show your partner you care?

Monday

_____   _____   _____

Tuesday

_____   _____   _____

Wednesday

_____   _____   _____

Thursday

_____   _____   _____

Friday

_____   _____   _____

Saturday

_____   _____   _____

Sunday

_____   _____   _____

MASTURBATION

Many of us have grown up with negative feelings about masturbation, resulting in a tendency to feel guilty or abnormal if we masturbate. Yet now we know that masturbation is perfectly normal and not in itself at all unhealthy. It is practiced by most people of both sexes and can actually teach us much about our capacity for gaining and maintaining erections.

You can do it in complete privacy and at your own pace. You don't have to worry about how you look or how your partner is responding and since you get immediate feedback, the learning occurs more quickly.

MASTURBATION EXERCISE 1

Stop/Start

Masturbate, using a water soluble, lubricant-like massage oil—Astroglide, olive oil, or whatever you prefer. Concentrate on the sensations you are feeling in your penis. **Once you have an erection, take your hand away and think about something else. Wait until your erection is completely gone, which may take a few minutes. Then start masturbating again.** If you are not able to regain your erection after a few minutes of stimulation, see if there is anything you can do to make yourself feel more relaxed and turned on. You might consider looking at an erotic book, sexy pictures, or a sexually explicit video tape. Again, if your penis gets hard, stop and lose the erection. If you're not able to get hard, just quit for the day and try again later in the week. Do this exercise for about twenty minutes, losing and regaining the erection twice if you can. Repeat this entire exercise at least two to four times. The object of this exercise is to increase your confidence that you can regain an erection under the right circumstances.

Day 1:   Date _____
Things that helped to regain erection: _____

_____

_____

Day 2:   Date _____
Things that helped to regain erection: _____

_____

_____

Day 3:   Date _____
Things that helped to regain erection: _____

_____

_____

Day 4:   Date _____
Things that helped to regain erection: _____

_____

_____

BAN ON INTERCOURSE

While you are gaining skills to help you with maintaining your erection, it is important to discontinue having intercourse with your partner so you do not keep reinforcing a pattern of erection loss during partner sex.

This, however, does not mean that lovemaking is off limits—only intercourse. You can participate in any other sexual activity you desire—in fact, expanding your repertoire of sexual pleasuring is important, so feel free to experiment.

We will get back to intercourse with specific exercises. Meanwhile, take this opportunity to branch out and have fun.

WEEK 3

SAY "NO"

Some men with erection problems find it difficult to set limits. They find themselves doing things they don't want to do—even having sex sometimes when they would rather not. In essence, their penis is saying no by not getting erect. One way to deal with this is to learn to say "no" to things—both outside and inside the bedroom.

Say NO to three things a day that you really don't want to do, but normally would agree to do. You can say NO to a request by someone else. Or you can say NO to yourself when you feel that you "should" be doing something.

List the three things you said NO to each day this week.

Monday

_____   _____   _____

Tuesday

_____   _____   _____

Wednesday

_____   _____   _____

Thursday

_____   _____   _____

Friday

_____   _____   _____

Saturday

_____   _____   _____

Sunday

_____   _____   _____

MASTURBATION EXERCISE 2

Switch-Hitter

While imagining any fantasy that you are comfortable with, masturbate using the hand you do not ordinarily use. For instance, if you regularly use your right hand, use your left or vice versa. It may take longer for you to reach a full erection using this technique, but it will provide you with a new set of sensations that can help you break any pattern of nonerection that you may have developed.

Repeat this exercise two to four times for at least 15 minutes per session.

Date   **What you learned from doing the exercise**

_____   _____

_____   _____

_____   _____

_____   _____

_____   _____

_____   _____

_____   _____

_____   _____

_____   _____

_____   _____

_____   _____

_____   _____

CARING MASSAGE

A caring massage is a pleasurable way to explore intimacy. It is not sexual, but an opportunity to get close and enjoy being together. The object is to soothe and relax, not to work out muscle kinks.

Prepare a comfortable environment where you won't be disturbed. Create your own world—just for the two of you. It doesn't have to be elaborate. Find a quiet room, close the shades, add some flowers, light a candle or two. Lie on the rug or on a firm mattress freshly made up with attractive sheets. Anywhere that you feel warm, comfortable, and secure will do. And don't forget a spill-proof bottle of oil; it's essential for a good massage. The oil should have a light, pleasant scent that you both enjoy.

Make sure you have everything you need—once you start you won't want to be interrupted.

As Giver: Spend 30 minutes experiencing and stroking your partner's body in a loving way that gives *you* pleasure. Don't emphasize breasts and genitals, but don't avoid them either.

As Receiver: Relax and enjoy the massage. If a certain kind of touching feels unpleasant to you, let your partner know in a positive way how it could be changed: For example, "A little more firmly, please—that tickles." If the touch is neutral or positive, simply relax and enjoy it.

After 30 minutes switch roles. Repeat this exercise on two separate occasions.

First Massage

Role as Giver: What you learned from doing the exercise

_____

_____

Role as Receiver: What you learned from doing the exercise

_____

_____

Second Massage

Role as Giver: What you learned from doing the exercise

_____

_____

Role as Receiver: What you learned from doing the exercise

_____

_____

WEEK 4

SAY "YES"

Say YES to yourself. Ask for, or let yourself have three things a day that you would really like to have. Make sure these are things you would not normally let yourself have or ask for. Begin small: Ask for help with a job you would normally do yourself, or treat yourself to a small gift, or 15 minutes in the sun.

If you feel guilty when doing this exercise—ignore that feeling!

Don't worry if you find yourself getting confused as to whether you are doing the "Yes" or "No" exercise. They're opposite sides of the same coin.

List the three things you said YES to each day this week.

Monday

_____   _____   _____

Tuesday

_____   _____   _____

Wednesday

_____   _____   _____

Thursday

_____   _____   _____

Friday

_____   _____   _____

Saturday

_____   _____   _____

Sunday

_____   _____   _____

MASTURBATION EXERCISE 3

Losing Erection Fantasy

This time, while you are masturbating, get hard and then fantasize a situation with your partner where you would normally lose your erection. Or, if you have a problem getting an erection in the first place, fantasize just being with your partner sexually. If you don't lose your erection with the fantasy, stop the stimulation. Then relax and do something within the fantasy to put yourself in a sexier frame of mind.

Fantasize in detail what you have to do to relax and then get excited again— a particular kind of stimulation or a certain activity that your mate could carry out. Imagine yourself asking your partner to do this for you. Continue masturbating while you visualize yourself regaining your erection. Imagine yourself having a fulfilling and enjoyable sexual experience. Repeat this exercise as often as needed to give yourself the confidence to do this in real life with your partner.

What are you doing when you lose the erection?

1. _____

2. _____

3. _____

What can you do that helps you relax and regain the erection?

1. _____

2. _____

3. _____

SENSUAL MASSAGE

A sensual massage can be an extremely erotic addition to your lovemaking. The combination of relaxation and arousal is hard to beat. So as you did with the Caring Massage, prepare a comfortable environment where you won't be disturbed. Sharing a refreshing shower together is sometimes a nice way to begin.

For this massage, you can spend a disproportionate amount of time on breasts, genitals and other sexually sensitive areas—but not before spending ample time on the rest of your partner's body.

Switch roles after 30 minutes or longer. Repeat this exercise on two seperate occasions. Erection can be a part of this exercise, but don't "try" to get one. In fact, try not to notice whether your penis is erect or not. (Remember, the ban on intercourse is still in effect.)

First Massage

Role as Giver: What you learned from doing the exercise

_____

_____

_____

Role as Receiver: What you learned from doing the exercise

_____

_____

_____

Second Massage

Role as Giver: What you learned from doing the exercise

_____

_____

_____

Role as Receiver: What you learned from doing the exercise

_____

_____

_____

WEEK 5

MASTURBATION EXERCISE 4

Sexual Options Fantasy

Make a list of five pleasurable things you can do with your partner during sex that is not dependent on your having an erection.

Begin to masturbate while imagining yourself in a situation where you are unable to have an erection. Stay with that thought for a moment and imagine yourself feeling OK about this. See yourself telling your partner that you are not going to have an erection this time.

While continuing to masturbate, visualize yourself doing one of the pleasurable activities you listed that does not require an erection. Imagine your partner and you having a pleasurable, sexy time together. As you fantasize her pleasure and yours, continue masturbating and reinforce this feeling of enjoyment. As before, if you get tense or anxious at any point just stop for a moment until you feel more comfortable and then continue.

Repeat this exercise as often as needed to give yourself the confidence that you could do this in a real life situation.

List the things that you can do during sex that don't require an erection:

1. _____

2. _____

3. _____

4. _____

5. _____

Now masturbate while visualizing doing one of these activities.

Date   What you learned from doing the exercise

_____   _____

           _____

           _____

_____   _____

           _____

           _____

_____   _____

           _____

           _____

_____   _____

           _____

           _____

CONDITIONS FOR GOOD SEX

Make a list of those things that make a sexual experience good for you. Ask your partner to make a similar list.

A few examples:

- Taking your time
- Oral sex
- Not being too tired
- Hard stimulation of your penis/gentle clitoral stroking
- A massage
- Certain music
- Soft lighting

Let this list be as long as you like—but make sure that you write down at least 10 items!

1. _____
2. _____
3. _____
4. _____
5. _____
6. _____
7. _____
8. _____
9. _____
10. _____

ENJOY THE MOMENT

For this exercise, it's helpful to have a watch with an alarm function. If you're at home use an alarm clock or a kitchen timer. Set your watch or timer to alert you once every hour.

Every time the alarm rings, stop and think about what you are doing at that very moment. How are you feeling? Could you add anything to the activity you are performing that would give you greater pleasure? Eating a meal slowly, for instance, and savoring every bite. Enjoying the wind in your hair as you take a walk. Even doing a job you don't like in the most efficient way possible so that you'll be finished more quickly.

Notice your enjoyment level every hour for one day and evening. The purpose of this exercise is to help you to focus on the pleasure of the moment and how to get the most out of it.

Activity	How did you make it more pleasurable?
_____	_____
_____	_____
_____	_____
_____	_____
_____	_____
_____	_____
_____	_____
_____	_____
_____	_____

WEEK 6

RESISTANCE

As you begin to make changes you may notice that you start to feel afraid. While consciously you may be convinced that you do not want things to stay the same, there is always a certain amount of fear of the unknown; the fear that if things change, they could become worse. If, and when, the fears start to win out over the desire to grow, you may neglect to do the homework, or feel that the assignments are irrelevant, or pick fights with your partner that make working on the problem impossible. But stick with it.

I cannot stress enough that you *will* feel discouraged along the way if real changes are being made. Don't let it get you down. Here are some ideas that will help you get back on track:

- If you need to, take off a day—or two days at most.

- Repeat some of the earlier exercises that were carried out successfully as a way of bolstering your confidence.

- Do the exercises for this week a second time. Suspend any negative judgements or feelings of failure. This is a process. The time-line will vary from couple to couple. Success is the result of tenacity. If you stick with the process, you *will* be successful.

- Use your own creativity. Create variations on the exercises to make them more relevant or appealing to you.

SHARING "CONDITIONS FOR GOOD SEX" LISTS

Earlier, you each made a list of those things that are most likely to make a sexual experience more enjoyable for you. Since everyone is different, you cannot possibly know everything your partner needs for a good sexual experience and your partner cannot automatically know what you need.

Share your Conditions for Good Sex lists to convey your sexual needs to each other. Talking explicitly about your sexual needs may provide new information for your partner. You may find that you've been touching your partner the way *you* would like to be touched as a way of communicating *your* preferences. Your partner, on the other hand, may be doing the same with you. Perhaps your preferences are quite different. Talking about them will go a long way toward clearing up the non-verbal *mis*communication.

CONDITIONS FOR GOOD SEX

Conditions that are different
For example: I like sex at night/partner likes sex in the morning.

1. _____
2. _____
3. _____
4. _____
5. _____
6. _____
7. _____

Conditions that you share
For example: We both prefer lots of time.

1. _____
2. _____
3. _____
4. _____
5. _____
6. _____
7. _____

Now brainstorm to add more items to the shared list.

8. _____
9. _____
10. _____
11. _____
12. _____

ERECTION PROBLEMS EXERCISES WITH PARTNER

You and your partner should read and discuss each of the erection problem exercises before starting them. Remember, your sex life will not be limited to these exercises forever, just for a short while until you can learn some new attitudes and methods and complete the program.

Work out an agreement with your partner as to the frequency with which you will do these exercises—two to three times a week is best. **Your partner should understand that it is important that you are in control during these exercises.** Her job is to respond to you and she shouldn't try to rush you or push you further then you wish. During this time no demands should be made on your penis. Feel free, however, to satisfy your partner with your hands or your mouth.

Make sure to incorporate some warm, affectionate, physical contact like cuddling or kissing at the beginning and end of each of these exercises.

PARTNER EXERCISE 1

Soft Penis Exercise

You and your partner should get into a position where you both feel comfortable. Let your partner stroke, caress, and play with your penis in any way that she likes. **Concentrate on the experience of being touched while your penis is soft. If you get an erection, stop and wait until your penis becomes soft again.** Then ask your partner to continue. Let her know if anything she does is uncomfortable or painful, but otherwise just relax and focus on the sensations in your soft penis. If you feel any pressure to get an erection, merely acknowledge those feelings. Then bring your attention back to your penis and the experience of having your partner touch you.

Repeat this exercise until you feel comfortable having your partner play with your penis while it is soft.

What you thought or noticed while doing this exercise.

EXAMPLE

Mar 7   I wonder if she feels turned off.
               I'm feeling embarrassed.
               My penis is more sensitive than I thought.

Date

_____   _____

         _____

         _____

         _____

_____   _____

         _____

WEEK 7

"I" MESSAGES

One of the most important communication skills to learn is the use of "I" messages.

Begin to use the words "I feel" when talking with your partner.

For example, "*I* feel unimportant when you're late for dinner and don't call," is much more effective than, "*You* don't care about anyone but yourself, or you wouldn't keep me waiting."

The "You" statement is a blaming statement, and will often start or escalate an argument.

An "I" statement reports your feelings and generally makes it easier for your partner to respond in a positive way.

Feelings are expressed by such words as: hurt, frustrated, lonely, inadequate, happy, loving.

Think of something your partner did that upset you and write how it made you feel—as if you were telling your partner at the time.

I feel _____ when you do/say _____

_____

Beware: Don't use "I feel" when you mean "I think." "I feel *that* you ..." or "I feel *as* though you ..." or "I feel *like* you ..." are thinking statements, not feeling statements. You are analyzing your partner, not expressing your feelings.

Think of something else your partner did that upset you and write how it made you feel—as if you were telling your partner at the time:

I feel _____ when you do/say _____

_____

COMMUNICATING PREFERENCES

Each person has unique sexual preferences. Your partner is not a mind reader. The purpose of this exercise is to let your partner know as much as possible about your sexual likes and dislikes.

Compile a list of all the ways you enjoy being touched. Be as specific as possible. For example: "I like to begin with light touches all over my body; I love my hair pulled as I get more excited;" and so on. Whenever possible, state each item in the list in a positive way. Rather than listing, "I don't like my penis stimulated right away," write, "I like stimulation of my penis best after I'm warmed up a bit."

In addition, make a list of all the sexual touches and activities you *think* your partner enjoys most. Then read each other's list and discuss each item in detail.

List the ways you enjoy being touched sexually.

_____

_____

_____

_____

_____

_____

_____

_____

_____

_____

List the ways you think your partner enjoys being touched during sex

_____

_____

_____

_____

_____

What did you both learn when you discussed your lists?

_____

_____

_____

_____

_____

_____

_____

_____

_____

PARTNER EXERCISE 2
Communicating Touch

Set aside an hour to enjoy each other sexually. **The object of this time together is to communicate what *you* enjoy sexually.** The only activity that is off-limits is intercourse.

At some point in this exercise show your partner how you like your penis touched. Do this by having her place her hand over yours as you stimulate yourself.

Then guide her hand, putting your hand over hers while suggesting the kinds of strokes, rhythms and pressures you prefer.

Both show her and tell her how you like to have your body touched, how you like to be kissed, how you like to be stimulated orally. Be specific. And be certain to let her know when she is pleasuring you in a way you enjoy.

Do this exercise several times. Don't worry if you do not get an erection. The object of this exercise is to communicate what you enjoy sexually.

Date   **What you learned from doing the exercise**

_____   _____

            _____

            _____

_____   _____

            _____

            _____

_____   _____

            _____

            _____

_____   _____

            _____

            _____

WEEK 8

ACTIVE LISTENING

When a disagreement comes up, most of us don't really listen to our partners because we are too busy preparing our own replies. To prevent this, try this simple exercise: Pick a topic that has caused a moderate amount of conflict in your relationship. Both partners should limit their statements to just a few sentences at a time. The person listening must feed back to the partner what he or she just heard the partner say before presenting his or her own point of view.

Both partners switch back and forth in this manner:

1. *He* makes a short statement expressing his point of view.
2. *She* repeats what she heard him say.
3. *He* agrees with her translation or corrects it.
4. Once she has repeated it back to his satisfaction, *she* succinctly states *her* own point of view. (*He* then repeats it as in 2, and so forth.)

Try "active listening" four times, alternating who picks the issue to discuss.

Date	Topic of Discussion	What you learned about your partner's point of view

PARTNER EXERCISE 3

Give to Get

Again, set aside an hour to enjoy each other sexually. Again, intercourse is off-limits. The object of this exercise is to divert the part of you that watches and judges the performance of your penis.

Begin making love in the ways you enjoy. **When you notice that you are evaluating the performance of your penis, silently tell yourself to stop. Then actively shift your attention away from your penis by focusing your attention on pleasing your partner.** Begin to touch her, orally and manually, in ways you know she enjoys. Each time you find yourself evaluating your erection, refocus on giving your partner pleasure.

List the pleasurable activities that took your mind off your penis:

Date   What you learned from doing the exercise

_____   _____

           _____

           _____

_____   _____

           _____

           _____

_____   _____

           _____

           _____

_____   _____

           _____

           _____

WEEK 9

ALWAYS/NEVER EXERCISE

Discontinue using the words NEVER and ALWAYS. As in, "You're *always* late" or "You *never* help me with the dishes." The problem with using these words is that your partner will focus on the exceptions and the point you are trying to make will be lost.

Most important, it is necessary to remember that the object is not to win the argument. If one person wins the other loses, and then both lose, because the loser will find some way to get even. Instead, the object is to understand your partner's point of view, to hear what his or her needs are and to take responsibility for whatever your part was in the conflict. This makes it easier to reconcile and let go. In the end it's a lot more fun to feel loving and close. Hard feelings and emotional distance are just plain painful.

For three days try to keep track of how many times you say "always" or "never" to your partner. Aim for zero.

Day 1	Number of times you said "always"	Number of times you said "never"
Morning	_____	_____
Afternoon	_____	_____
Evening	_____	_____
TOTAL	_____	_____

Day 2		
Morning	_____	_____
Afternoon	_____	_____
Evening	_____	_____
TOTAL	_____	_____

Day 3		
Morning	_____	_____
Afternoon	_____	_____
Evening	_____	_____
TOTAL	_____	_____

PARTNER EXERCISE 4

Stop/Start with Partner

Once you are comfortable, ask your partner to stimulate you manually or orally. Again, intercourse is off limits. **Once you have attained an erection, ask her to stop stimulating you. Then wait until your penis gets soft. When your penis is completely flaccid, ask her to begin stimulating you again.** If you achieve a second erection, stop and lose it one more time. After that, you're on your own.

You may not be able to get an erection when doing this exercise or you may have one erection and then not be able to regain it the second time. Don't let this worry you. Just tell your partner that you're not going to get hard this time. Then initiate one of the five pleasurable activities you listed when completing the Sexual Options Fantasy exercise in Week 5.

Whether or not your penis responds, it's important for both of you to know that you can still have a good time together.

Repeat this exercise several times.

Date   **What you learned from doing the exercise**

_____   _____

            _____

_____   _____

            _____

_____   _____

            _____

_____   _____

            _____

WEEK 10

EROTIC LITERATURE

Reading erotic literature can build sexual energy. Buy a sexy magazine or an erotic book* that has a style you enjoy.

For a minimum of five days, read a few pages of the magazine or book at least three times a day.

Also, read some erotica in the evening after dinner, especially if you think there's a chance you may be carrying out Partner Exercise 5 (the next exercise).

Day 1: Date _____   Erotica read: _____

time _____ time _____ time _____ time _____

Day 2: Date _____   Erotica read: _____

time _____ time _____ time _____ time _____

Day 3: Date _____   Erotica read: _____

time _____ time _____ time _____ time _____

Day 4: Date _____   Erotica read: _____

time _____ time _____ time _____ time _____

Day 5: Date _____   Erotica read: _____

time _____ time _____ time _____ time _____

*An erotic literature reading list is on the following page.

SOME GOOD EROTIC LITERATURE

By Lonnie Barbach
Pleasures: Women Write Erotica
Erotic Interludes: Tales Told by Women
The Erotic Edge: Erotica for Couples

By Anais Nin
Delta of Venus
Little Birds

By Nickelson Baker
Vox

By Susie Bright
Herotica I, II, & III
The Best of American Erotica, 1993, 1994, 1995, 1996

Classics
The Story of O by Pauline Regea
Lady Chatterly's Lover by D.H. Lawrence
Fanny Hill by John Cleland

PARTNER EXERCISE 5
Quiet Vagina

Your partner's vagina should be well lubricated with KY jelly or Astroglide before beginning this exercise.

Lie on your back and ask your partner to sit on your thighs, facing you. Let her stimulate your penis in any way that you suggest. Let her rub your penis in her pubic hair and then against the lips of her vagina. **When you feel ready, ask her to insert your penis into her vagina very slowly until it is totally inside of her. Now just stay still for a few moments and focus on the sensations you feel in your penis.** Then, when you are ready, ask her to move her hips in a gentle, rhythmic, nondemanding manner while you simply enjoy it. This is merely a practice exercise, not one designed to achieve orgasm for either of you.

If at any time, you would like her to stop moving for a minute or discontinue the exercises completely, it is important for you to feel free to ask her.

Repeat this exercise several time until you can contain your penis in her vagina comfortably for 15 minutes.

Date   **What you learned from doing the exercise**

_____   _____

             _____

             _____

_____   _____

             _____

             _____

_____   _____

             _____

             _____

_____   _____

             _____

             _____

WEEK 11

STATE OF THE UNION EXERCISE

Set aside an hour to talk with your partner about your relationship. Share your feelings on the positive and negative aspects of the preceding week. You may want to talk about specific exercises from this program or other ways you've thought of to spice up your sex life.

End the discussion by letting your partner know three things that he or she did for you during the previous week that you particularly appreciated.

Schedule a "State of the Union" appointment for the next week. This exercise should be carried out every week until it becomes an integral part of your relationship.

Meeting Date _____   Time _____

Negative aspects of preceding week _____

_____

_____

Positive aspects of preceding week _____

_____

_____

Three things you appreciated about your partner this past week

_____

_____

_____

Three things your partner appreciated about you this past week

_____

_____

_____

Next meeting:

Date _____   Time _____

WEEK 11

PARTNER EXERCISE 6

Pelvic Pleasuring

Repeat the Quiet Vagina exercise in its entirety. Then as you begin to feel comfortable being quietly contained inside your partner, ask her to slowly increase the pace of the thrusting. If you would like to, you can slowly thrust also. But keep in mind that the object of this exercise is to experience pleasure, not to attain orgasm. Striving to satisfy your partner or to reach orgasm yourself—so as not to "waste" the erection—only puts more pressure on your penis to perform. Orgasm will occur quite naturally as you become more comfortable with having your penis inside your partner's vagina.

Repeat this exercise as often as you need to until you are comfortable with full movement.

Date   **What you learned from doing the exercise**

_____   _____

            _____

            _____

_____   _____

            _____

            _____

_____   _____

            _____

            _____

_____   _____

            _____

            _____

WEEK 12

TRY SOMETHING NEW

Don't let the day go by without trying to add at least one new thing to your love life. It can be as simple as kissing your lover somewhere you never have before—on the neck or inner thigh. Or as elaborate as designing an evening with all the props you can find—from satin sheets to sex toys. Read to each other; play with each other; talk to each other; act out a fantasy. A good sexual relationship requires time, planning, and preparation. Love and intimacy can grow stale when taken for granted. When was the last time you said, "I love you"?

What did you add to your love life this week?

Monday: _____

Tuesday: _____

Wednesday: _____

Thursday: _____

Friday: _____

Saturday: _____

Sunday: _____

BACKSLIDING

If you've experienced significant positive changes, don't be alarmed when some backsliding takes place from time to time. **It is important to realize that a certain amount of backsliding is a natural part of any growth process.** Your sexuality may be a sensitive area and particularly susceptible to outside stresses or especially vulnerable to difficult periods in your relationship. By keeping your sexual relationship prioritized, backsliding is less likely to occur. If it does, simply repeat the series of exercises that have been most helpful to you.

List the exercises that have been most beneficial for you:

_____

_____

_____

_____

_____

_____

_____

ACKNOWLEDGMENTS

Many of the sexual exercises and THE CONDITIONS FOR GOOD SEX EXERCISE were developed by Bernie Zilbergeld, Ph.D., author of *THE NEW MALE SEXUALITY*.

SAY YES, SAY NO, and BACKSLIDING were adapted from *FOR EACH OTHER: SHARING SEXUAL INTIMACY* by Lonnie Barbach, Ph.D.

FOREPLAY and STATE OF THE UNION come from *GOING THE DISTANCE: FINDING AND KEEPING LIFELONG LOVE* by Lonnie Barbach, Ph.D. and David Geisinger, Ph.D.

CARING DAYS is borrowed from the work of Richard Stuart, D.S.W.

Thanks to Claudia Vagt for her help with the writing and editing of many of the exercises and to Marilyn Anderson for her assistance in organizing and typing the manuscript.